SECOND EDITION

Storybook 13

The
Boot Book

by Sue Dickson

Illustrations by Norma Portadino, Jean Hamilton, Chip Neville and Kerstin Upmeyer

Printed in the United States of America

Modern Curriculum Press, an imprint of Pearson Learning
299 Jefferson Road, P.O. Box 480, Parsippany, NJ 07054
1-800-321-3106 / www.pearsonlearning.com

ISBN: 1-56704-523-5 (Volume 13)

I J K L M N—CJK—10 09 08 07 06

Table of Contents

Raceway Step 26

2

A Trip to the Zoo

Vocabulary

1. zoo
2. booth
3. room
4. pool
5. too
6. stool
7. boot
8. goose
9. hoop
10. cool
11. pool
12. stoop
13. poor

14. mood
15. noon
16. soon
17. sooner
18. fool
19. food
20. scoot
21. roof
22. spoon
23. moon
24. goofy
    bal loon
25. balloon

Story Words

26. other
27. mother
28. ticket
    an i mal
29. animal
30. animals
    al most
31. almost
32. bears
33. polar bears
34. wäter
    zoo keeper
35. zookeeper

3

"Here we are at the zoo," said Janet.

"We can buy our tickets at this booth," said Fred. "This will be fun for us. The animals have lots of room to play in this zoo."

"See the seals swimming in that pool," said Janet. "They do tricks, too. See that one up on the stool. He has a big yellow balloon. Look at that one on the rock with a boot !"

"They **are** funny," said Fred.

"See the seal tooting a horn," said Fred.

"Look at the one jumping in and out of a hoop," said Janet. "There are the polar bears, too. They like the cool water in their pool !"

SPLASH !

"They are funny clowns,"
said Fred. "They like to
fool each other. See
them stoop down and
then jump up in the cool
water. Look out, Janet !
They will fool you, too !"

7

"Look at that poor tiger !" said Fred. "He seems to be in a sad mood !"

"Maybe he wants some food," said Janet. "It is almost noon. Maybe the zookeeper will feed him soon."

8

"What a goofy monkey!" said Janet. "He can scoot up to the roof!"

"Here comes the zookeeper with some food," said Fred.

The man fed the monkey. Then he said, "Did you ever see a monkey eat with a spoon?"

"No," said Fred.

"Let's go into the Children's Zoo now," said Janet.

"Look! That monkey is pointing the way with his spoon," giggled Fred.

Janet and Fred went
into the Children's Zoo.

"There is the cow that
jumped over the moon,"
said Fred.

"Here are the three mice," said Janet. "Their home is a boot!"

"That is funny," said Fred.

"Here is Mother Goose. Do you think she will tell us a story?" asked Janet.

What a happy day Fred and Janet had! A day at the zoo is fun!

The End

13

The Loose Tooth

Vocabulary

1. booth
2. school
3. mood
4. soon
5. food
6. smooth
7. smoothed
8. goose
9. cool
10. coop

11. stoop
12. loop
13. poor
14. toot
15. stool
16. shoot
17. fool
18. noon
19. loose
20. root
21. choose

22. proof
23. tooth

   tooth paste
24. toothpaste

25. school

26. shoe

<u>Story Words</u>

   morn ing
27. morning

28. apple

29. Mrs.
(Mis iz)

14

Tom Booth is six years old. He is in the first grade at school.

One morning Mrs. Booth went up to Tom's bedroom and said, "Get up, Tom! You must go to school soon. You have to get to the bus stop on time."

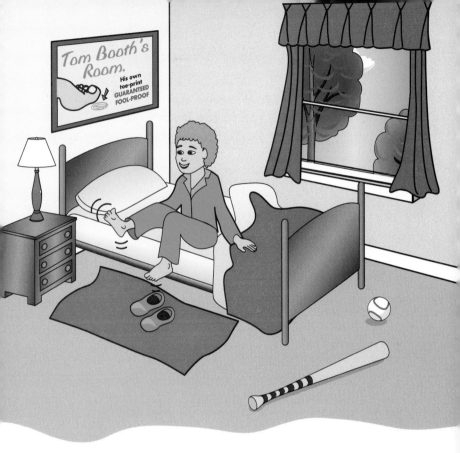

Tom was in a fine mood. He jumped up from bed.

"OK, Mom, I'm up !" he said. Then he got dressed for school.

Tom ran to his mom in the kitchen. She had fixed his food. Tom sat in the booth to eat it. He had one egg and some toast. He smoothed butter on his toast.

18

Next, Tom ran out to the back yard to feed his pet goose. He gave her some cool water.

Tom had to stoop to tie his shoe. The lace had come loose. He made a big loop. Tom did it! Tom is a big boy!

Tom had to rush to get to the bus. Poor Tom must run ! Here comes the bus !

Just as the bus started,
a puppy ran into the
street. He ran in front of
the school bus !

"Toot, toot," went the
horn of the bus. The
puppy ran away.

When Tom got to school he had the best time ! He sat on a stool to play "Pop the Balloons." The boys and girls in his class clapped when Tom said, "o͞o !" You cannot fool Tom ! Tom is smart.

23

At noon the boys and girls had lunch. They ate in the lunchroom at school.

Tom ate a big lunch. He drank some cool milk, too. Then he bit into his apple.

"$\overline{OO}$!" said Tom. "I have a loose tooth!"

25

Tom looked at his apple. What was **that** ? It was his big, loose tooth ! It had stuck in his apple !

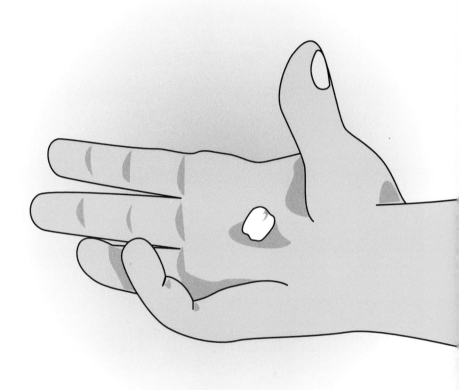

"Come see!" said Tom. "My loose tooth came out! I did not use a tool! My apple got it out for me!"

The boys and girls looked at Tom's tooth. It had a big root on it.

Rick likes to fool and joke. He said to Tom, "Why don't you glue it back in with toothpaste?"

The kids giggled.

When Tom got home, he ran to tell his mom. "See my tooth !" he said.

"Fine !" said Mrs. Booth. "The tooth fairy will have to come see you soon."

When Tom went to bed
he put the tooth under
his pillow.

30

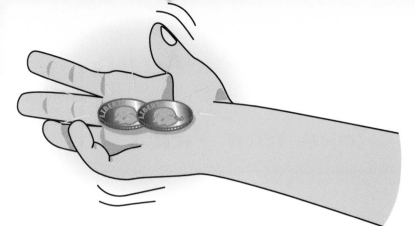

In the morning Tom yelled, "See what the tooth fairy left for me! Fifty cents! I am in a fine mood! I will tell the kids at school!"

"I hope Miss Fix will choose you first!" said Mom. "Show and Tell will be fun for you today!"

"Yes, it will!" said Tom with a grin.

The End 31

A Book, Hook-A-Fish, or Paint... Take Your Pick !

Vocabulary

1. book
2. books
3. look
4. wool
5. cook
6. hood
7. brook
8. hook
9. wood
10. stood

11. foot
12. shook
13. Brooks
14. good
15. crooked

Story Words

16. wänt
17. wänts

what ever
18. whatever

Miss Brooks said, "It is time to choose. You may choose whatever you want to do in school."

The kids clapped. They liked Choosing Time at school.

Bill, Patty, Kim and Donna went to the book shelf. Bill wants to look for a book. Patty, Kim and Donna want to look for books, too.

Bill took a book. So did Kim. They sat down to look at them. What is Bill's book about? What is Kim's book about? Patty will choose a book soon. What will Patty choose?

35

Steve and Ann picked a
game. The game has a
brook and a pond. It
has five fish and two
poles with hooks. The
game is "Hook-a-Fish."
Steve and Ann have fun
with it.

Jenny, Sally and Brad choose the big wood blocks. Jenny stood on the "B" block. Sally stood on the "S" block. Brad stood on the "V" block. He stood on his left foot. Now he will hop to the rug.

37

"May we paint?" asked Paul.

"Yes, if you choose," said Miss Brooks. "You may choose to do whatever you wish."

Then Paul, Judy and Janet started to paint.

Choosing Time at school is fun.

38   **The End**

Our Nation

Raceway Step 26B

tion

Vocabulary

1. nation
2. election
3. station
4. information
5. condition
6. action
7. pollution
8. attention
9. constitution
10. foundation
11. celebration
12. vacation
13. dictionary
14. expectation
15. question

Story Words

16. who

17. birth day
    birthday

39

The United States
of America

The U.S.A.
is our nation.

In the U.S.A. we choose
our leaders. We choose
them on Election Day.
We go to vote.

Our leaders speak on TV stations. They give us information. They tell us about the condition of our nation. They tell us what they will do. They ask us to vote for them.

The leaders tell us we must take action to stop pollution.

Our leaders tell us to pay attention to the laws of our nation.

The laws of the U.S.A. are in a list. The list of laws is called the Constitution.

The U.S. Constitution
was a new invention. It
was made by the leaders
who started our nation.
The laws of the
Constitution give us
freedom in the U.S.A.

On the Fourth of July
we have a celebration.
It is during summer
vacation. It is the
birthday celebration of
our nation.

You may have a question about the U.S.A. You can look in a history book or in a big dictionary. We are proud of our nation, our Constitution and our freedoms.

The End

The Neighborhood Costume Party

Vocabulary

1. knight
2. bright
3. light
4. fright
5. frightening
6. fight
7. bought
8. doughnuts
9. taught
10. eighteen

11. thought
12. brought
13. might
14. weigh
15. neighbors
16. neighbor hood
neighborhood
17. straight
18. enough

Story Word

19. Dr. (doctor)

It was the day of the neighborhood costume party. Mark was dressed as a knight. His sister, Maria, helped him get dressed. The sun was bright in the sky. Mark will help Maria. He will go out to get the party food from the neighbors. 49

Maria will decorate the party cake. She has candles to make the room pretty and bright.

It is time for Mark to go out to get the party food. Maria will give him a bag to put it in.

I'm a knight too! My armor keeps me safe all my life, all day, all night!

"Hold on to your bag, Big Knight," said Maria.

Mark waved to her and went down the street. He held the bag in his hand.

"It is tight in my hand," he yelled back to Maria.

Soon Mark met Mrs. Peck's daughter, Jenny. She was dressed as a little Pilgrim girl.

"Hello, Mark," said Mrs. Peck's daughter.

"Hello, Jenny," said Mark. "Do you want to help me? I am going to pick up the party food from our neighbors."

"Yes," said Jenny.

Mark and Jenny went along in the neighborhood. They went to Mr. Jones' house.

"Do you have a treat for the neighborhood costume party?" asked Mark.

"Here you are," said Mr. Jones. "I brought home some doughnuts for the party."

"Thank you, Mr. Jones," said Mark and Jenny.

"Your mothers taught you good manners," said Mr. Jones. "You are welcome. I hope you like the doughnuts. What nice costumes you have ! The neighborhood party will be fun."

54

Next they saw a frightening sight... two cats in a fight !

"What a fright," said Jenny. "I'm glad you are with me, Big Knight !"

Then they went to Dr. Mink's house, number eighteen, Straight Street.

"Hello Mark. Hello Jenny," said Dr. Mink. "Here is the popcorn I bought for your party. I thought you might like it. Here are some apples, too."

"Mmm ! Thank you, Dr. Mink," said Jenny and Mark. "We have such good treats. You are a nice neighbor !"

"I am glad your mom taught you such good manners," said Dr. Mink. "Have fun at the costume party."

"Well, our bags weigh a ton ! That's enough for us ! Good-bye, Dr. Mink," said Jenny and Mark. "Our neighbors are nice, and our costume party will be fun ! Let's hurry to it !"

The End

The Tough Knight

Vocabulary

1. daughter
2. sleigh
3. neighborhood
4. naughty
5. eighty
6. bright
7. fright
8. neigh
9. neighed
10. fight
11. taught
12. ought
13. mighty
14. knight
15. fought
16. caught
17. frighten
18. bought

19. cough
20. coughed
21. tough
22. rough
23. enough
24. thro͞ugh

Story Words

25. terrible
26. palace
27. dragon

57

One day King Tweek's daughter, Ann, was riding in a sleigh through her neighborhood.

All at once...

...a naughty dragon
jumped out at her!
He was eighty feet long!
He could cough a big
bright fire!

Poor Princess Ann got a terrible fright! Her horses neighed and ran back to the palace.

King Tweek called for a tough knight to come and fight the dragon.

The dragon ought to be taught a lesson !

It was a mighty battle ! The knight and the dragon fought for eight days !

The knight caught the
dragon by the tail. The
dragon fell on a big
rough rock !

"Enough ! Enough !"
coughed the dragon. "I
have thought about it.
I will not frighten King
Tweek's daughter again !"

The dragon went on through the town. He went to live in the hills.

Good-by ! I will never frighten anyone again ! You have taught me it is better not to fight !

Princess Ann and the tough knight had a big wedding. They bought a house in a pretty neighborhood. They were very happy.

64   **The End**